R U B A N K   E D U C A T I O N A L   L I B R A R Y

SELECTED STUDIES

Advanced Etudes, Scales and Arpeggios in all Major and Minor Keys

H. Voxman

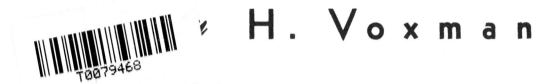

ADVANCED ETUDES

SPECIAL STUDIES

SCALES AND ARPEGGIOS

RUBANK®

HAL•LEONARD® CORPORATION
7777 W. BLUEMOUND RD. P.O. BOX 13819 MILWAUKEE, WI 53213

C Major

HEINZE

Copyright MCMXLII by Rubank, Inc., Chicago, Ill.
International Copyright Secured

Molto allegro

A Minor

Allegro brillante

LUFT

5

MÜLLER

Moderato assai *(in 4)*

F Major

FEDOROW

HEINZE

D Minor

HEINZE

Allegro furioso

G Major

MÜLLER

Allegro moderato, ma brillante

E Minor

HEINZE

FERLING

Allegro moderato con fuoco

B♭ Major

HEINZE

FERLING

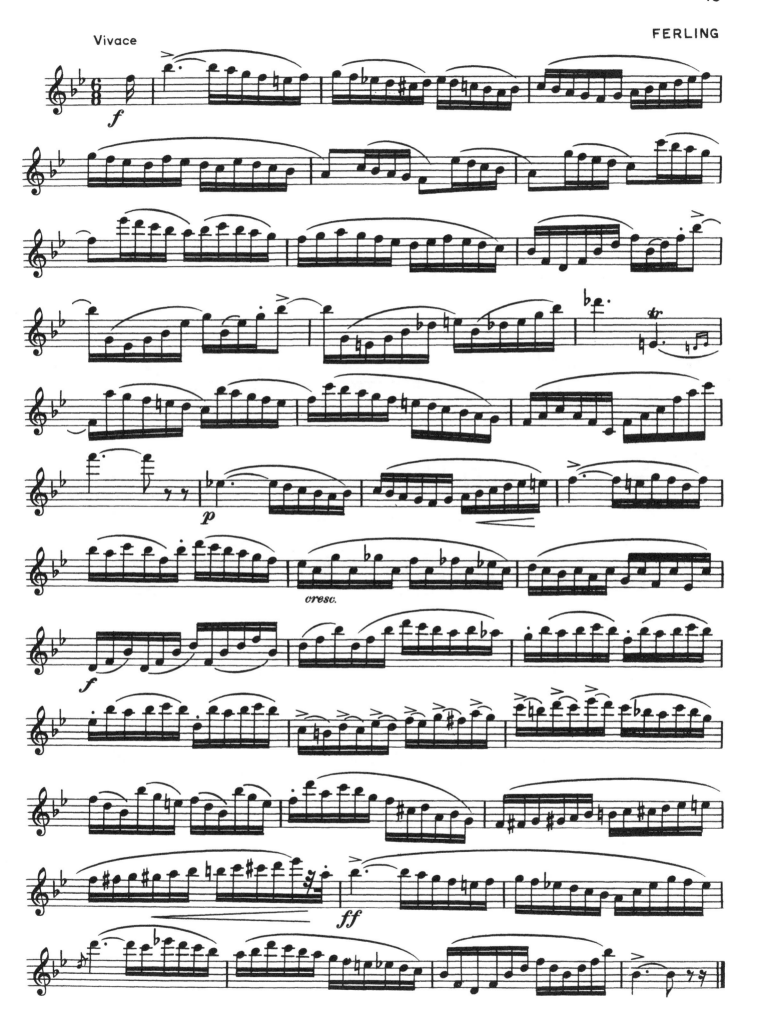

G Minor

Andante con moto

LUFT

D Major

FERLING

Andante con gusto

B Minor

DROUET

GAMBARO

Eb Major

HEINZE

Tempo di marcia

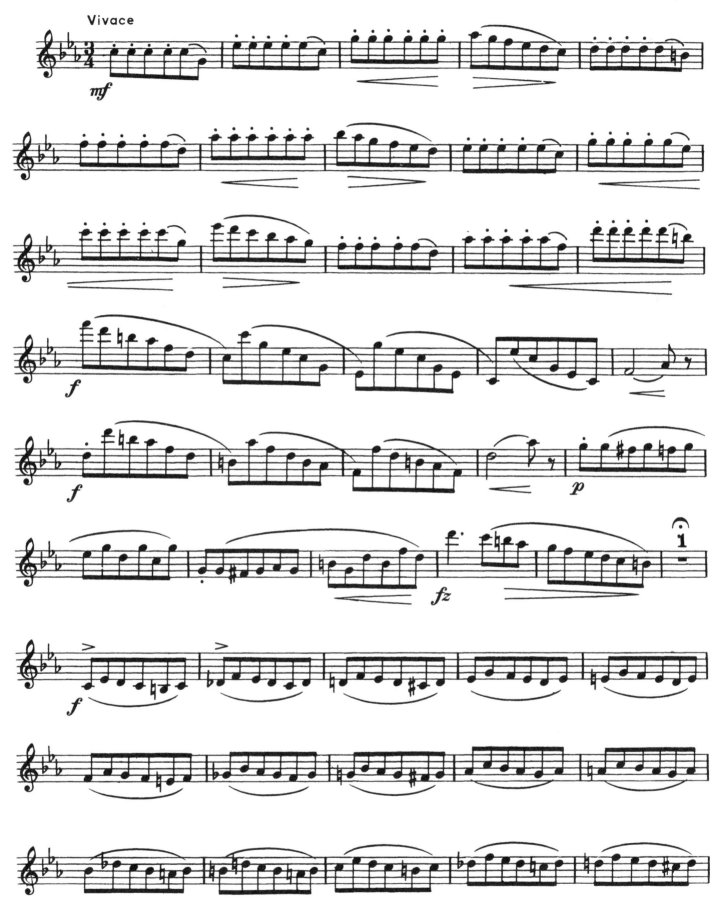

C Minor

LUFT

HEINZE

Adagio (in 8)

A Major

FERLING

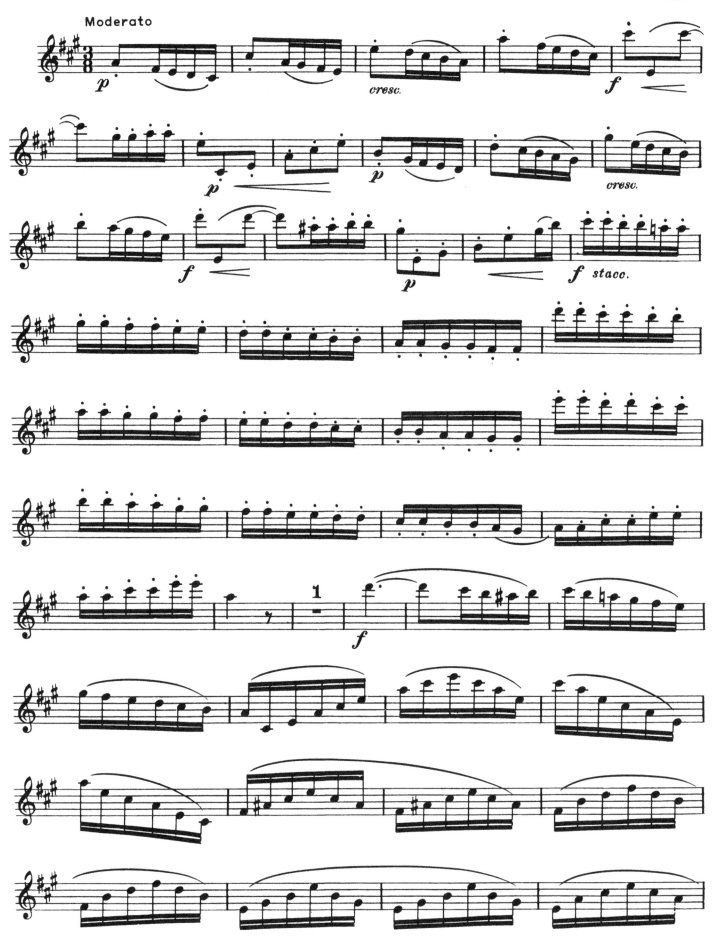

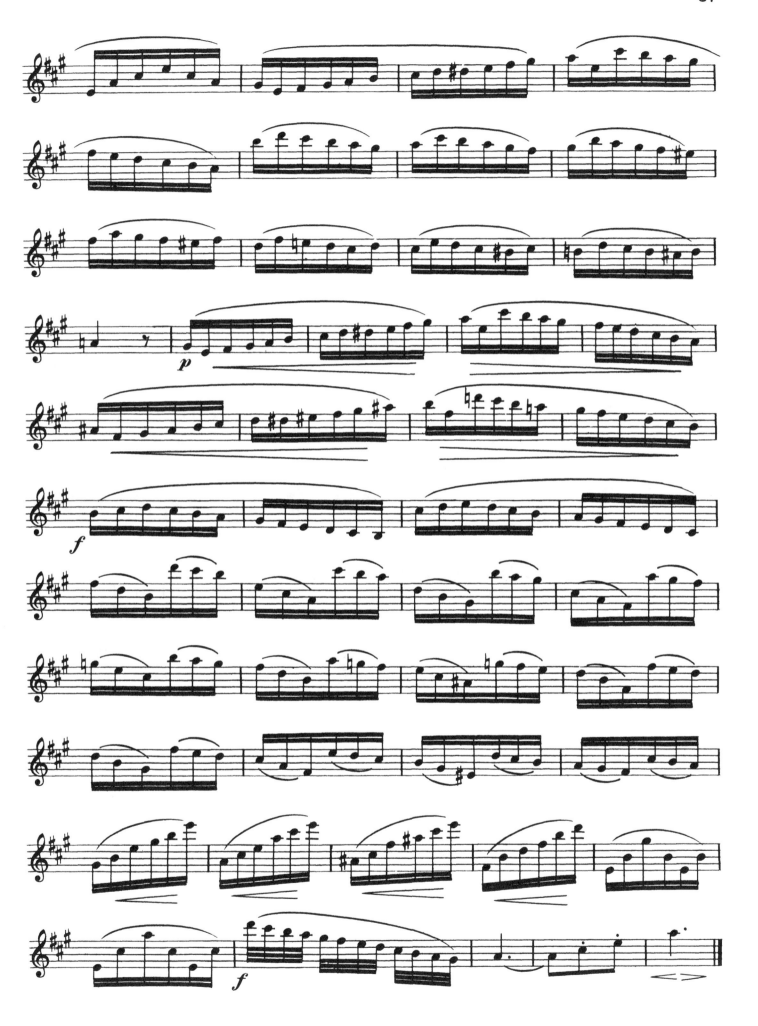

F♯ Minor

Andantino (in 6)

HEINZE

LUFT

Allegro marcato

A♭ Major

LUFT

FEDOROW

Andante sostenuto

morendo

F Minor

PAESSLER

Andante cantabile

Scherzo

E Major

HEINZE

FERLING

Allegro poco moderato

C# Minor

FERLING

FERLING

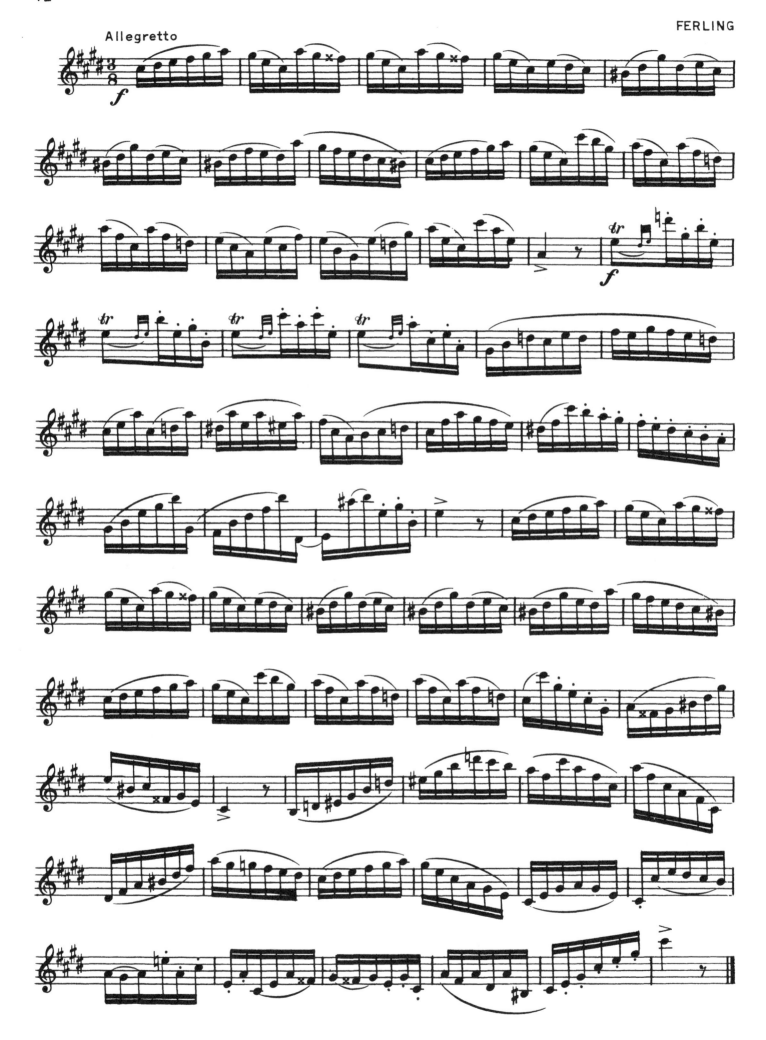

D♭ Major

LUFT

44

Poco allegretto (in 1)

FERLING

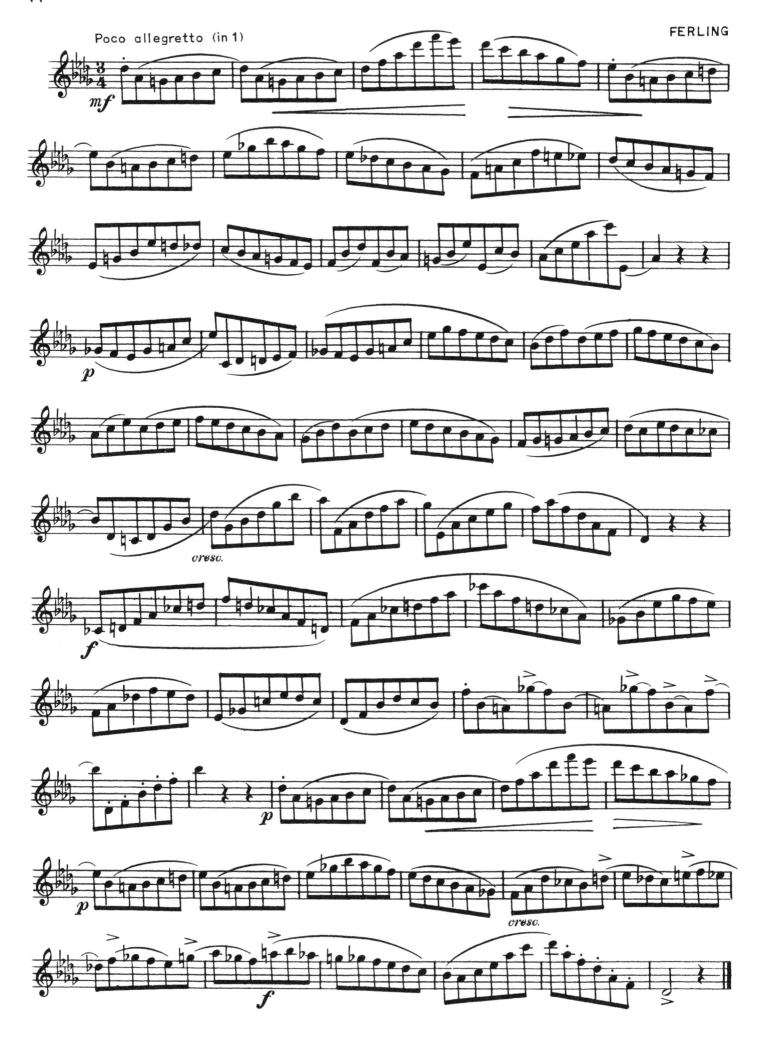

B♭ Minor

LUFT

HEINZE

Allegretto

B Major

FERLING

Maestoso (Allegro)

Allegro

HEINZE

G# Minor

Scherzo

HEINZE

Allegretto

FERLING

G♭ Major

HEINZE

51

HEINZE

E♭ Minor

HEINZE

FERLING

F# Major

HEINZE

Andante sostenuto

HEINZE

Vivace

in sharp rhythm

D# Minor

DROUET

58

HEINZE

Interval Study

KREUTZER - ROSE

Allegro assci

Chromatic Etude

Allegro vivace

HEINZE

Scales

The use of a metronome with the following exercises is highly recommended.

C Major

A Minor *(melodic form)

F Major

D Minor

G Major

* All minor scale exercises should also be practiced in the harmonic form.

Copyright MCMXLII by Rubank, Inc., Chicago, Ill.
International Copyright Secured

62

E Minor

Bb Major

G Minor

D Major

B Minor

63

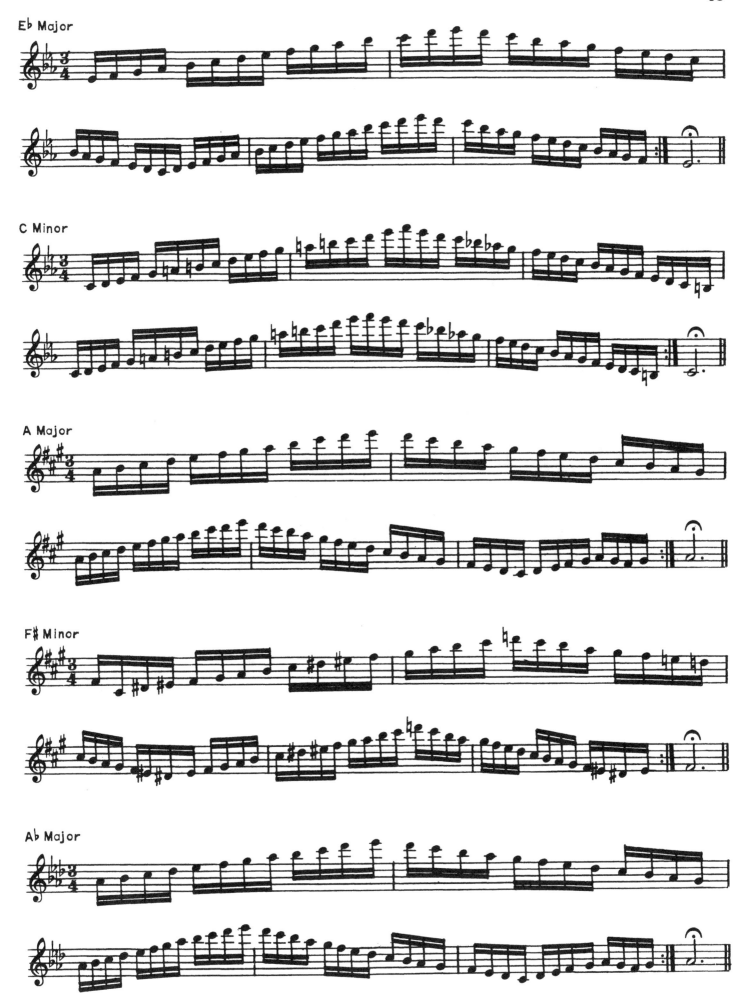

F Minor

E Major

C# Minor

Db Major

Bb Minor

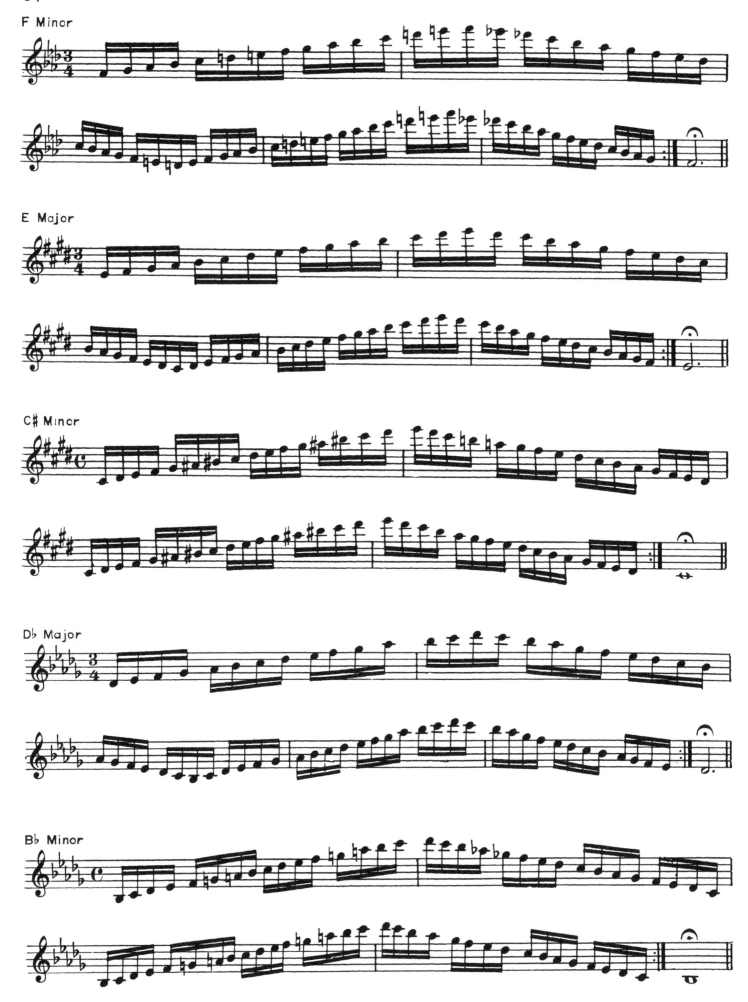

65

B Major

G# Minor

Gb Major

Eb Minor

F# Major

66

D♯ Minor

Whole-tone Scale on B♭

Whole-tone Scale on B♮

Chromatic Scales

Scales in Thirds

C Major

A Minor *(melodic form)

F Major

Copyright MCMXLII by Rubank, Inc., Chicago, Ill.
International Copyright Secured

68

D Minor

G Major

E Minor

Bb Major

69

G Minor

D Major

B Minor

E♭ Major

C Minor

A Major

F# Minor

Ab Major

F Minor

E Major

C# Minor

Db Major

72

Bb Minor

B Major

G# Minor

Gb Major

Eb Minor

F# Major

D# Minor

Major thirds

Intervals derived from the whole tone scale.

Minor thirds

74

Arpeggios

C Major

A Minor

F Major

D Minor

G Major

E Minor

Bb Major

G Minor

Copyright MCMXLII by Rubank, Inc., Chicago, Ill.
International Copyright Secured

Db Major

Bb Minor

B Major

G# Minor

Gb Major

Eb Minor

F# Major

D# Minor

Arpeggio of the augmented 5th on C

Arpeggio of the augmented 5th on Db